Things They Don't Tell You

Markell Sorp

MPW LLC

Contents

Chapter One

Introduction

Growing up, I learned a lot from the people around me. Whether they be friends, family, teachers, or a complete stranger, everyone has something, an experience, or point of view that may change your perspective. Despite the vast amount of information we process and should be learning from every day, there are still pretty big gaps in our practical knowledge when we become legal adults, which is at 18 years old where I live. For some reason, the people we are closest to and rely on the most as we grow up tend to leave out a lot of their wisdom and knowledge when deciding what to pass on to us. I'm not saying that they're doing this on purpose; not always at least. Many times, our parents and teachers simply never think to mention some of the things discussed in this book. Other times, this information may be left out because they themselves don't know enough about the subject.

That's not really the point of this book. The point of this book is to outline the things my peers wish they were taught to this point in their lives. More specifically, I'll be keying in on things that probably should have been taught to us from either our parents or teachers (including college professors). I couldn't tell you how many times I've come across something in adult life where I felt pretty unprepared. I don't think it has to be this way as often. Given how many interactions there are between the experienced adults and the young adults, it is sort of unacceptable how many things have been skipped over, especially in schools. Why is there an economics class that only teaches us business economics? How many students will go into a profession where their macroeconomic and microeconomic grasp on their market will make a difference in their performance? These are the questions I want to ask to those who make the curriculums, the people who claim to want to make a difference with the youth.

This is just one of the many ideas that will be discussed in this book. I interviewed 6 of my peers from graduates from average high schools with no college experience to private high school and private college graduates. Sure, you could say the sample size is too small, but I doubt that the result of the interviews/research would be much different over 10, 50, or even 100 interviewees. If anything, there just may be more data to show what should be focused on the most. In all reality, everything that my interviewers brought up is valid and should be addressed in one way or another for everyone in that transition into adulthood.

I know that a lot of high schoolers won't read this, especially if it's assigned reading. The same goes for college students in their first year or two. The contents of this book should be just as important for those students as it is for their teachers, professors, and parents. Knowing information that they may be lacking as they enter adulthood should be enough for the people who possess that knowledge to realize that they should pass it on. The goal here is just to help more people feel prepared to enter adulthood, whether that be in college, the workplace, or in general.

Chapter Two

High School

Introduction

While Kindergarten through the end of middle school are important to form fundamental knowledge and social skills, high school often is the most important schooling to prepare you for becoming an adult. Of course, many people become legal adults while in high school, but they often continue to live with their parents and exhibit many of the same behaviors that they exhibited in the years prior to turning 18. I'm not really here to criticize that or to say that people should automatically change their behavior the second they turn 18. The point here is that school systems should be well aware of what age groups are in elementary, middle, and high school, and tailor their curriculum to prepare the students for what they know is coming next. It's important to note that not everyone who's in high school will go to college or even finish high school. This is something that the people in positions of power should hold very central to their management of high schools. In my experience, high schools are dead set on "preparing you for college." The problem with this is that colleges offer hundreds of majors that will be explored by the hundreds to thousands of students that come out of any one high school. How could any one high school possibly expect to prepare those students for their individual major selection? On top of that, many students change majors in college. Proof of the lack of preparation to even enter college is that many students have no idea what they even want to major in on the way to college. So what are high schools really trying to prepare you for?

High School Academics

I think it's pretty clear and obvious that academics are the most emphasized part of the high school experience. There are different clubs and athletic groups that are available, but once again, those are all optional, and the vast majority of students opt out of joining. In the interview process, the difference between a public high school and a private one highlighted that although private schools may invest more time and effort into the individual student, at the end of the day, it's clear that those students feel like they are very well prepared to take standardized tests. The interviewee who attended a private high school recalls that while he never had to study entering high school, he quickly realized that his grades were slipping in high school. His teachers decided to help him and tutor him, which helped him learn to write and study more effectively. He was the only person I interviewed who was taught to study in his time in school before college. Now, I'm not trying to say that only private schools teach studying skills or provide one-on-one tutoring, but I don't think that it would be a stretch to say that it would be more common in private schools. So, that's one thing that high schools need to spend more time on: teaching studying skills.

Now, most of the other interviewees decried the lack of specialization in preparation to enter college. One said that K-12 exposes students to many different subjects, but he still didn't feel prepared to choose a major or career at the end of it all. He would later go on to explain that the academic jump from high school to college was pretty large to him because college courses were so much more in depth than high school courses. A current Stanford student said that while he thought that K-12 did a decent job in terms of academics, he still needed a lot of time in college to determine what he really wanted to do. Yet another interviewee explained that the structure of K-12 was "very rough on a young mind" and that it "imprisoned his creativity." With all of this taken into consideration, it shows me that most high schools don't do a good job of thinking ahead for their students. As I explained earlier, there are hundreds of major options in college, which everyone employed in the education system should be well aware of. Yet, many students aren't prepared to make the choice of major. The Stanford student even switched majors once in college, taking the dramatic leap from physics to English. Students should be given the opportunity early on to take a deeper dive into different subjects and explore different fields. Not only would it help them decide what subjects they really care about and which ones they really don't like, but also give them a head start on the major selection process and what they will eventually study. At the core of it, the rigid coursework that many high schools put in place hurts students' ability to explore and really find out what's right for them. As far as academics go, I think that most high school curriculums are far too broad from beginning to end to truly prepare the average student for college. Perhaps the first couple of years can be broad to polish up some foundational knowledge and skills. After that, I think the majority of coursework could benefit from being more elective-based, where students can explore different fields to find what they might want to learn more about in college.

High School Social

Everyone's high school experience is different, some more than others. I think it's safe to say that while there are people who are not social at all and people who are extremely social, most people are somewhere in the middle. Personally, the social aspect of high school is the most important part. As discussed earlier, this level of education doesn't do the greatest job of helping students prepare for their career or degree, so the least it could do is help them develop their social skills. Despite the clubs available to many students, the variety is often lacking, with not enough diversity to cater to everyone. This isn't to say that everyone should be catered to and there should be a club for every niche, but there should be more than what there is. At my school, students could recommend new clubs to be added, which then had to be approved, which sounds nice at first until you realize how many limitations the school puts on these clubs.

One interviewee wishes "there were more real-life applications of the things [he] learned." I agree that this should be incorporated into the curriculum during class, but having a wide range and variety of clubs would not only help students explore different fields and find out what they really have an interest in, it would likely also provide some more real-world applications of what was taught in class. On top of that, being in a club, you will get experience interacting and working with people in a more realistic setting. What I mean by this is that in your day-to-day life, you're not in a classroom. Most people are in an office or some other workplace learning as they go, applying what they know and have learned. It's hard to get that social experience in the classroom. The way most classrooms work made another interviewee get the feeling "there was a system or protocol for everything," and everything was bureaucratic. While some workplaces and situations are bureaucratic, many aren't, which that interviewer would later explain that his workplace and college experience shattered that idea. The Stanford student flat out said that high school could do a better job socially, bringing up clubs specifically. Better club selection and management could really help students prepare for both college and work. Giving them the opportunities to work on extracurricular projects more autonomously without classroom restrictions would give them a great head start on their way to the 'real world'. I know that it's difficult to recreate "client interactions," something one interviewee who works in personal finance deals with daily, at school or in a club, but just having less structured time to work on projects you care about with your peers goes a long way.

Okay, so not everything social is related to college or work prep. This is where I think most high schools do a passable job. Friend groups naturally form in this part of most people's lives, and many of them last for a fairly long time. It is probably just a product of a bunch of people of a similar age being together for a larger portion of their waking hours, but where or how else would it get done? These non-academic or project-based interactions between students are just as important for their well-being, if not more. Most people need to have some sort of social intelligence to have friends and acquaintances, and most people want to have and keep friends and acquaintances. In high school, we learn what we can and can't get away with in relationships and how to keep them strong. Of course, there are mistakes made, but that's a great way to learn what not to do. No one I interviewed complained about this social aspect of high school. The opportunities to form low-to-no-pressure relationships in this stage of your life are good enough for most people, and I can't really recommend any changes here.

High School College Prep

As I touched on a little earlier, I think it's fairly obvious that many high schools prioritize college prep over many other aspects of student life. While I explained that high schools do a dismal job of helping people choose what field to pursue, there are other aspects of college that some of my interviewees brought up. As both high school and college focus heavily on tests with very similar structure, the interviewers felt that they were well prepared to handle college tests. This makes sense. Although most high schools do not provide much practice for many practical things, they sure do provide more than ample practice for tests across many different subjects. Similarly, the interviewer who went to a private high school also felt that high school prepared him for college very well. Interestingly, the interviewer who felt that high school gave him the impression that everything had a protocol also said that despite feeling stifled creatively in K-12, those years still prepared him well for college. He compared his experience in high school to a build-up of creative potential energy that was essentially released in college, helping him think more freely. I found that very interesting. I wouldn't expect that experience would be looked at in a positive light, making someone feel prepared for the next step.

At the end of the day, most of the gripes my interviewers had with their high school preparation for college had to do with their preparation for real-world experiences. In college, you have much more freedom in your free time than in high school, but you aren't given any tips or guidance on how to use it. Further, there isn't any preparation for the financial aspects of college, either. One of my college classmates explained that he wishes that high school both gave better examples of the applications of the things we learn, which would help people choose a field and understand why it is or isn't important in day-to-day life. A breakdown on financing college would be helpful, too. He would go on to say that he thinks that most students take on student loan debt thinking that it's normal and necessary. The Stanford student also said he was overwhelmed with the amount of freedom that he was given in college. High school could certainly simulate more and more freedom throughout the 4 years of the experience, which I think would really help many students transition to not only college but also adulthood. In the grades leading up to college, there's just not much focus on anything that you will experience once it's over. There's no wonder why many people switch majors and end up in jobs that have nothing to do with their degree.

High School Work Prep

Not everyone goes to college, so this part is just as important as the others. So many jobs these days will not hire you without a degree, which is quite unfair in some cases. It's important that those who decided to get money now, rather than later, can do exactly that without turning to shady means. With the emphasis that high schools put on preparation to enter college, they tend to overlook preparing people for getting a job. My school was a little different, requiring students to have an internship for two semesters of their last two years, which does give students an idea of what a workplace is like. Not every school is like this. Even despite the internship experience, one of the people I interviewed who went to my school said that he didn't feel like that experience prepared him all too well. In his field, his interaction with his clients is very important. Most interns just never get to the point of interacting with clients. Now, I'm not saying that interns should get thrown into that fire, but I am saying that schools should try to sprinkle some of these experiences into their curriculum or at least teach some aspects of it.

The classmate of mine who said that his creativity was stifled also felt like high school did a poor job of preparing him for entering the workforce for that exact reason. As an architect, he needs to be creative and having everything laid out in such a structured way contradicts his current workflow. A couple of interviewees brought up that high school is also lacking in a lot of the technical information for many jobs, which is partially a product of trying to teach everyone essentially the same broad subject matter for 13 years. However, they understand that it would be difficult to do anyway with so many fields and interests. On top of that, many jobs teach you the more technical things on the job, so it isn't as much of a big deal as some other aspects.

While my school had us build a resume in preparation for our internships, the Stanford student still feels like it wasn't enough. Another one of my classmates noted that there's a big difference between what is on a resume and the person whose credentials are on it. I think it would be easy to have a more comprehensive professional skills course for a semester that really dives into what skills you need to land a job. Sure, a solid resume is one thing, but interviewing is just as important, if not more. Most of us don't put every single skill, experience, and outlook on a resume, so the interview can really boost some candidates' position amongst other applicants. Another thing that an interviewee brought up was negotiating pay. This was a great idea in my opinion. Perhaps it would be better suited for college, but even some colleges don't teach that. Every student coming out of high school should be armed with the knowledge of how to properly bring up the subject and negotiate. Even with this being said, I will say that part of the work-prep problem is on the employers who won't even look at a candidate without a degree, as if going to school for longer will make someone a better employee and team member.

While this may not be the best place to bring up this issue, as it's not necessarily an issue with most high schools, I think it is important to be said. Companies should really start considering people without a college degree more seriously. I've been told that a degree shows that someone can stick to something for a long time, but what does 13 years of grade school do? You spent your time learning about things that didn't interest you and tested well enough to graduate high school. How is that less valuable than 2 to 4 years of more specialized learning that often doesn't even translate to most real-world jobs? Plus, most high school days are 7-8 hours long, while many college students may have that many hours of class in a week. High school certainly tries to push everyone to go to college, which I will give them credit for. However, not everyone can afford it. Others just aren't cut out for that kind of structure, even if it is less structured than high school. Employers should invest in training their employees whether they have a degree or not. In all honesty, someone fresh out of college with a bachelor's degree doesn't have much of a leg up on someone who just graduated high school in certain fields. As I touched on earlier, most jobs are far more niche than what a bachelor's degree is able to teach you, so most of what people end up learning for work is picked up on the job. Maybe you would be more familiar with a couple of concepts if you graduated college, but let's be honest. A good number of us largely forget many concepts once finals are over. I just find it puzzling that something as trivial as a degree can essentially bar someone who has all of the other qualifications and experience from getting a job.

High School What They Got Right

So, it seems like High School could certainly be better in a variety of ways. Is there anything that should remain the same? Honestly, there were very few areas where my interviewees felt that High School prepared them well for their future. The only thing that came up multiple times as a positive for High School was that it helped prepare them for test-taking in college. Yeah, it kinda sounds like a joke. However, if we break it down, there may be a silver lining. The structure of most High Schools, although stifling and unrepresentative of the real world, did allow for one interviewee to find ways to develop ways to stay focused. That is something that can really help people as they transition into college and the workforce.

I also want to add that I think the social aspect, although flawed, is more right than wrong. The relationships and interactions you have with both teachers and classmates are one of the closest things to real life there is in High School. What I mean is that it's very rare to run into a social situation at or through school that wouldn't happen as an adult. Through trial and error, you learn how to interact with people more effectively and not stick out as a weirdo. Still, this isn't perfect, as most of the day your teachers are pretty much wanting you to sit and listen without much socialization. If schools can find a way to make learning more experiential, I think a lot of problems would be solved.

That's really the solution to a lot of my interviewees' problems with High School. They want to learn about things they will actually experience in life. As I said, after middle school, you've learned just about everything the average adult knows when it comes to common math, writing, and reading skills. High School should be tailored to help students do a few things:

1. Fine-tune Social Skills: Give people the chance to work to-

gether as much as possible. Let them form and test different relationships, but in realistic scenarios. Group projects kind of do this, but there's room for improvement.

2. Figure out what they want to do: Instead of having students continue to take mandatory classes they don't care about, let them explore different fields and disciplines until they find something they're really interested in. There are more majors than math, science, social studies, and language arts/English. Students should be exposed to as many disciplines as possible and be encouraged to explore. One or two electives is really not enough. Maybe half or more of the classes a high schooler takes should be chosen by them and not mandatory. I think this will help people figure out what they want to do in college and after.

3. Teach them things useful in real life: This is probably the biggest shame of most modern high schools. The fact that I can be working and driving at 16, but know nothing about filing taxes, personal finance (credit cards, mortgage, rent, student loans), and insurance is absolutely a systematic failure. Schools are so focused on having your standardized test scores look good that they push aside what really matters. Who cares if I can analyze *The Great Gatsby's* theme if I don't understand my car insurance agreement? Why do I need to know an integral of a function but not how to calculate how much house or rent I can actually afford? For the people who work in the education system and claim that they care about the children and the future, it's a shame that they leave your buildings not only feeling, but being woefully unprepared for life outside of them.

College isn't there to hold your hand and teach you these things. Once you're in college, everyone's going to tell you you're an adult. Even high school teachers tell you that it'll be different in college. Yet, they willingly let you leave knowing you tested well enough to graduate with a not very well-rounded foundation. Yes, it's a lot of work to fix these things. Maybe what I've suggested isn't the answer, but neither is what most kids 18 and under have now.

Chapter Three

College

So, I just put a lot of pressure on grade school, especially high school. I think they deserve that pressure. College is better, but could still use some work. Ideally, college should be a place that prepares you for the workforce and helps you adjust to a life with greater responsibilities. Granted, not everyone actually lives on campus, so it kind of becomes more like an extended high school experience with less workload for some people. As I've said earlier, a lot of what people learn in an associate's or bachelor's is really just the basics of what is used at whatever company or profession students end up in. This isn't to say that this information isn't important, but it just may be a little overrated in some cases. For certain professions, college is almost invaluable. It all really just depends on who you are and what your goals are. Unfortunately, high school very rarely does you any favors in helping you find what you actually want to do so that you go into college prepared. It's pretty often that people switch majors or end up working in a field unrelated to their major. Perhaps the academic material people learn in college is actually secondary to something else. Let's see if we can find out what that is.

College Academics

In my interviews, it was rare to actually hear anything about the academic aspect of college. One interviewee who switched majors from physics to English had high hopes for what college could do for him once he graduated. After speaking to him recently, it seems like the academic part of his experience was really more in the background than the foreground. I think this is reflected in the absence of standardized testing in college. Professors have a lot of control over the material that is taught and what is tested. I'm no expert in how colleges decide what is taught in what class, but I never got the feeling that there was a centralized body outside of the college mandating that x or y is taught and tested. I feel like professors often emphasize real-world examples and experience over the pure material. This is obviously in contrast to high school, which wanted you to test well over just about anything else. I didn't get the impression that any of my interviewees really had any qualms about the academic aspects of their collegiate experience.

College Social

The unique structure of college is something that all of my college-going interviewees appreciated. Whereas high school teachers were almost dictatorial, college professors are actually often more flexible and reasonable. One interviewer likened professors to a manager or boss at a company and the classmates to co-workers. I thought this was actually pretty accurate to my experience in mechanical engineering where there were a lot of group assignments and projects. We would be tasked with solving a problem by the professor with a lot of freedom in regards to how it was solved. Then, we would communicate amongst ourselves to figure out how to best proceed. I'm sure other majors are structured similarly in some classes. I believe this is where college shines. The freedom and greater opportunity to work with classmates toward the same goal simulates many workplaces in a variety of industries.

College Work Prep

Now, here's where I think people have the most problems and praise for college. As I was starting to touch on in the previous section, certain majors do give students a taste of what a workplace may be like. Something that came up in multiple interviews was professional development. I think this is the primary purpose of college.

In most cases, the primary reason people go to college is in order to get a well-paying job in their preferred industry. If college isn't successfully doing this for the majority of people, it is failing. Despite the actual material you learn in college being very broad and basic in the first 2 to four years, most of my interviewees acknowledged that college gave them opportunities to network and learn how to speak and present themselves in a professional manner. The college I went to has a Co-Op program, where students would use a semester to have an internship instead of having classes. Someone I went to school with reflected positively on that experience, noting that it gave them a preview of what life would be like after graduation. More specifically, they felt that it helped him form good time management and scheduling habits. Another one of my classmates largely echoed this sentiment, but was careful to point out that he learned a lot more niche details in his internships than what was ever brought up in the classroom. He said that he feels like on-the-job experience was the best way for him to learn.

The interviewees who didn't have Co-Op programs didn't have as much positive to say about what college did to prepare them for joining the workforce. One went as far as to say that he doesn't need a degree to do what he does now. Sure, he also told me that he essentially did the bare minimum in order to graduate and only completed his bachelor's degree for his mom, but I think his opinion is still valid. College did very little for him as far as his current position, as he created value on his own. He decided to get his real estate license on the side and ended up finding the finance industry on his own. He felt like college wasn't providing him with any value. Another interviewee could only speculate on what his college experience would do for him after graduation, expecting to be unsurprised by what companies may request of him and to be pretty certain of what he would do after graduation. However, once he graduated, and after switching majors, he still isn't certain what he wants to do. I'm sure his college experience influenced his decision to switch majors from physics to English, but with him trying to decide between a couple of routes in Buddhism I'm not sure it quite finished the job.

Still, these young adults still felt like college was missing a few things. The architect was disappointed that college only prepared him to work for others instead of giving him any pointers on starting his own firm. Further, they focused more on interactions with other architects instead of communications with clients. Another interviewee wishes he had been informed more about the various tests and certifications that he could get that would set him apart. That leads me to something that one of the people I went to school with brought up. Keep in mind that we had that Co-Op internship program where we had to develop a resume to land internships. He didn't feel like the course that we took going into those internships did enough to help him when it came to non-internship jobs. He specifically brought up that he wishes he had been taught about negotiations in interviewing. It's easy to get taken advantage of as someone new to the workforce and end up getting paid less than you're worth.

College What They Got Right

While I go over what my interviewees believe college did well, keep in mind that I went into this believing that it is meant to prepare people to join the workforce. In all honesty, it became pretty clear to me that the people I interviewed didn't really think that college itself really helped them in preparation for adulthood or work. What really helped them was the experiences that came with college. No one brought up the coursework as being helpful. What caught my attention was the opportunities that being in college provided these people with. Let's touch on a couple of examples. The architecture student really valued the opportunities he had to network and visit architectural firms as a student. Both of these things may seem like something you could easily do outside of a college setting, but if you're not super outgoing and not in college, I think you would find it challenging. The two interviewees that I went to college with felt that the Co-Op internship experience was very valuable. Specifically, they both appreciated the taste of what a work-life balance would be like once they graduated. They learned how to manage their responsibilities, money, and time.

The problem here is that not every school pushed their students to do an internship or have a truly experiential experience. Even then, some majors, and even students, work better than others when it comes to an internship. What's at the root of what these people liked about their college experience is that it gave them the opportunity to develop professionally. Now, I think that most of these people are more outgoing than average, so it was easier for them to take advantage of those opportunities. Perhaps college should do more to put students in the position to have those more experience-based situations rather than mostly classroom-based ones. I know that every curriculum is different and that students handle the workloads differently, but if the curriculum was structured more like what a job in that field would be like instead of lectures, I feel many students would feel more prepared to join the workforce and be on their own. As mentioned earlier, what you learn in the classroom is often tangential to or completely irrelevant to what a job may specialize in. Doesn't it make sense to get students ready to be in a setting where they have to learn on the job? Grade school should've given you the basics in math, reading, and writing. College should give you the basics of whatever field you're in while getting you comfortable in the settings that you may end up in. Somehow, college sometimes felt almost just as obsessed with test-taking as high school. There are very rarely tests at a job. Your performance is the test. Let students perform rather than recall and repeat. It'll help them develop problem-solving strategies that employers will greatly appreciate.

Chapter Four

Parents, Friends, and Family

Whether you realize it or not, most, if not all, of what you learn actually comes from the people you grow up with and around. These are the people who help to make you who you are. Everyone would be more or less the same if school taught them everything they knew. Despite all of what I've discussed to this point, I'm beginning to think that your parents, friends, and family might be the most important people when it comes to preparing you for life to come. When it comes to parents, they've been there before. They know, or should know, what it takes to be a well-adjusted adult in today's world. Knowing what they know, they should do their best to teach and prepare their kids. Surprisingly, it seems parents leave out a lot. Maybe it's because they weren't taught it, so the cycle continues. Or, perhaps it just gets lost in all of the other things they try to impart in their child. In any case, I want to help bridge the gap so that more people feel more confident in their early adulthood.

Life Skills

This is where I feel like your parents are most valuable in your early adulthood. Sure, I've been tough on K-12 and even college, but they shouldn't be held accountable for everything. There are certainly some things that parents need to teach their children. After listening to my interviewees, it's clear that when it comes to life skills, they want to be taught some of the same things they wanted from their high school. Specifically, the finances of being an adult and beyond are things that people often learn later in life, when they are already behind. The interviewee that I've known for the longest brought up investing specifically, which is a great example of this. The earlier you start saving and/or investing, the more you'll end up with, just because of time. This is something that should be emphasized at a relatively young age. The sooner the better.

Some other things that I want to touch on here weren't brought up by anyone I interviewed, but I think they are important. Personal hygiene is something that I feel some people think is self-explanatory, but it really isn't for some. When some people go from getting bathed to bathing themselves, not everything carries over. I know some kids will pretend to take a bath/shower just so they can do something else. While you may not think that behavior would transfer to high school age and beyond, habits start young, whether good or bad. Sure, they may eventually voluntarily bathe, but how well are they really doing it? Bathing isn't the only aspect of hygiene that needs to be more deliberately taught. Oral, facial, pubic, and even hair hygiene can easily go overlooked. Obviously, most people know they should brush their teeth twice a day and floss daily, but like bathing, if that habit isn't formed early, it can easily not form at all. This is usually just a problem with flossing, but the way you brush your teeth matters, too. As you grow older, some areas of your body need specialized attention. I'm talking about the pubic region and your face. As far as the pubic region goes, for men, just take a little extra time and care to clean thoroughly in all areas. I'm sure the same goes for women, but this is something that you should ask your parents or doctor for pointers on. As for facial care, for the longest time, I just washed my face with water and used regular body lotion as moisturizer. While this works just fine for some people, there are specialized face washes and moisturizers that can help with oiliness, dryness, and acne. It wasn't until I was out of college that I discovered and began to use these products. Also, you should wear sunscreen daily, not just when you go to the beach or pool, to keep your skin looking healthy for as long as possible. Finally, some hair types are easier to care for than others. Parents, who are likely to have similar hair to their offspring, should give their children tips and tricks to maintaining and styling healthy hair. What products should and shouldn't they use? Are there any methods they can use to style it quickly with minimal damage? If you know, don't be afraid to let them know. I know it took me a while to figure out what my hair did and didn't like.

Social Skills

In your youngest years, your parents should be teaching you what is and isn't socially acceptable. In my experience, most people do an acceptable job at this. I definitely feel like the time in high school and college really helps to fine-tune one's personality and behavior, but parents definitely set the groundwork. A couple of my interviewees actually brought up interactions with the opposite sex as it relates to what they were taught. One actually wishes his father taught him what makes a man and how to interact with women. He said that he often put himself in a more feminine and submissive way when he was around women in his high school years. This is something that I feel like many men have been seeking more and more guidance on recently. Just having more guidance as a young man in today's world could really benefit many of them. Now, I'm not sure how things are on the other hand, as my sole female interviewee didn't mention anything on this topic and I am a male, but I'm sure women could benefit from similar guidance from the older women in their lives. The other person that brought up the opposite sex said that the way his parents interacted with each other taught him how to act in his romantic relationships. This is very important, as I'm sure we've all heard of cycles of learned abuse. Setting a good example for your children in this aspect of life can put them on the right track down the road.

Miscellaneous Skills

This is where the bulk of comments were made about what was learned from the people in the lives of my interviewees. They talked about a little bit of everything from speaking and language to life philosophies. Of course, every family is different when it comes to the values they impart to their members, but it's important that this is done well. Sometimes those lessons end up backfiring, resulting in someone who has undesirable personality and behavioral traits. The Stanford student wishes his parents had taught him the value of hard work. While he admits that they may have said it before and he just may have forgotten, I think it shows that perhaps it wasn't driven home enough. He went on to expand on that idea by saying that he only recently realized that finding something that he was passionate about was the hard part in working hard. If he had something he truly cared about, he would have no problem working hard on it.

Unfortunately, because of the way most school systems are set up, he never really had the time or thought to think about and focus on what he really cared about until recently. He thinks if his parents had taught him this, he might be better off.

Another one of my interviewees often finds herself giving what in retrospect feels like too much of herself. She wishes that she was taught that not everyone is who they appear to be. Sure, most of us know not to trust strangers, but even people with whom you grow close can end up turning on you. This one has a fine line in it. On one hand, you don't want to be always on edge and suspicious of people, but you don't want to be taken advantage of, on the other. I suppose there may be some way to teach how to tell the difference, but nothing is guaranteed 100% accurate. Curiously, this same interviewer says that she learned that people can change for the better from her parents. I can only speculate, but perhaps learning that led her to hold out hope on people who are showing the signs of being two-faced. This goes back to being careful about what is taught and how it is taught. When you're young, it's easy to see things as black and white and not be able to grasp that there is nuance.

Something else that was brought up by one of my college classmates was the idea that life gets harder as you get older. This is more of a personal viewpoint, but I think there's some value here. Obviously, you're expected to take on more responsibility as you get older, and some of those responsibilities require you to provide value to the world in some way. Depending on who you are and what opportunities are available to you, you may end up in a situation you're not happy with. It's perfectly fair to see this as being harder than when you were dependent on your parents for your livelihood and little was expected of you. The tradeoff here is personal freedom. I think that's something that should be explained to young adults, if not to people even younger.

Maybe don't phrase it in those exact words, but let them know that the responsibilities will come and that the parent won't always be there or able to have their back. The sooner this is known, I feel like, with a combination of a few other things, we can find things and ways to make that transition easier and more pleasant than it is for many now.

What They Got Right

Everyone is different when it comes to what they value and what their goals are, so it makes sense that the topics in this section have and will continue to vary. I would recommend that you use this 'What They Got Right' section, not as things that you shouldn't have to worry about, but as inspiration for things that you definitely should teach if you're a parent. If you're a child, do the same, but ask for guidance from those in your life who you feel may be able to provide you with insight.

The basics are pretty well covered according to my interviewees. Many of them brought up language as something taught to them by their parents. This type of learning is both direct and indirect. Most parents teach their children letters, numbers, and some basic words. Children often pick up on basic grammar and other words by listening to their parents and family. Even in something as simple as speech, how it is taught matters. Most parents don't want their kids saying bad words and the like. A couple of my interviewees actually know multiple languages, as they come from Asian and European backgrounds. While this is just a product of who they are, some parents don't teach their children languages other than English, even if they speak something else themselves. I feel like even being basically conversational in more than one language is a very valuable skill, so

I encourage parents who are multilingual to pass on as much as they can.

Cooking is something else that came up multiple times in my interviews. While I love that this is something that is still taught in the home, I know that a lot of people these days don't know how to cook much other than instant ramen and scrambled eggs. Teaching your child something that literally has bearing on their ability to survive is invaluable and should be made a point to do when raising a person. Further, as parents come from different backgrounds, they can pass down some of their familial recipes and culture. Cooking is a great way to keep family traditions alive and go a long way to develop closer bonds. Who doesn't like a good meal, after all?

Speaking of culture and traditions, a few of the parents of the people I interviewed made it a point to set examples in those respects. Outside of food, multiple people brought up the fact that their parents taught them traditions related to their ethnic backgrounds. One went as far as to say that those lessons taught him to be a generally clean person. This same person also went on to say that although he didn't pray often when living with his parents, seeing his father do it often would lead him to follow suit once he moved out. In a similar vein to culture, general life mantras and ideals were also instilled in the people I talked to. Being raised by a single, hardworking mother taught one of my college classmates to not complain, as things could always be worse or more difficult. One of my classmates from high school also reflected on general character traits and ideas, like not complaining, that his parents taught him. He also remembers specifically that his dad often told him to be observant; something he only recently has taken to heart. Being a child of someone who was self-employed taught another about the entrepreneurial spirit and showed him that you can do just about anything if you put the effort in. He also mentioned that his family really was family first, not allowing things out of their control to impact their day-to-day life and demeanor. Even relationship skills were observed and learned by another person. I think all of these things illustrate that most parents really do care to raise someone well. There are a lot of things to teach someone, and it can be hard to get it all out, especially when many households have two working parents. Peers can sometimes help fill in some of the gaps, but they too are often lacking all of the tools they'll need as adults. Further, some interviewees brought up struggles with peer pressure even when they knew right from wrong. This isn't to say friends are bad by any means. Several instances of positive lessons have been learned from the friends of the people I spoke with. Most of them had to do with dealing with stress, having fun, and building a sense of camaraderie, all of which are important. What really matters when it comes to learning from friends is that the base at home has been built strong, so that peer pressure doesn't lead young adults down the wrong path. If those values haven't been taught effectively at home, it will be easy for them to be tossed to the side when the parents aren't there to supervise.

The sample size is pretty small, but I think most parents do a lot right. However, there's a lot to teach, so there are still blind spots. I don't expect parents to know and teach every single little detail about everything their child may encounter as an adult. The hope here is that with the knowledge of what young people say they're missing, they make the effort to fill in more of those gaps. Just asking a high schooler what they want to know may seem like an easy way to solve this problem, but I know from experience that you don't know what you want to know until you need to know it. You can never be too prepared for something, so never stop teaching your child. They may find it annoying in the moment, but they just might appreciate it later on.

Chapter Five

What We Would Teach Our Children

O K, we've gone over the good and bad of the systems and people that young adults go through on their way to adulthood. If we were parents, what would we be teaching our children? Well, I asked that, too. Everyone is a little different, but there were a few themes that came up multiple times.

General life and social skills were the most common lessons my interviewees wanted to teach. Independence and individuality came up a few times. It's pretty clear that many young people today are followers, copying what they see from their peers and online. Honestly, this isn't a very desirable trait, as it makes it hard for anyone to stand out from the crowd. Further, creativity and the ability to think for themselves were brought up, as well. Sure, it's fair to have similar opinions to others, but it's not great to just copy others' opinions and bandwagon certain ideas or concepts. Being able to think critically and form your own thoughts based on the information available is an invaluable skill. It really reduces the chances you will be manipulated. Being more of an individual, especially if pushed from a young age, can potentially help them figure out what things they are good at and what they like to do. This exploration can definitely put them at an advantage later in life when they're going to college and entering the workforce. Of course, almost everyone said something about money. Investing, taxes, and general personal finance are all things that we would teach our future kids.

Self-care and safety were next up. One person I spoke to even went as far as to say that they would get their child into martial arts for general self-defense. Getting children into sports and exercise early was brought up by two people. Another person mentioned teaching meditation and philosophy, which I don't think is a bad idea, as long as it's done well at the right time. Giving young people a way to deal with stress, whether it be through exercise or meditation, can set them up for success as they gain more and more responsibilities. A life with good mental and physical health is typically a fairly safe life.

Surprisingly, morality and doing what's right only came up once explicitly. Religion is another way that morals came up, but that's more of an indirect application of morality. I'm sure all of them would teach morals in some way, but I was surprised that it wasn't emphasized as much. Specifically, leadership and responsibility were the things that were touched on when it came to morals. A leader has greater responsibility than a follower, and no one wanted to raise a child who is a follower. Honestly, I think that as time goes on, this aspect of raising children will need to be emphasized more and more, as it seems people are beginning to do more and more immoral things in order to get ahead. That, paired with what seems to be a growing number of followers, calls for some course correction.

There are a few things that I want to add here that my interviewees didn't touch on. I would really want to teach my children things that they are more than likely to need to know at some point in their life. So, things like buying and registering a car, renting an apartment, and buying a house, are all things that I would teach them about. Sure, they may not be things that they would need in their first 18 years of life, but knowing the basics of each one of these things can help them plan for the future. Going into these things with any misconceptions can be pretty costly. How to take advantage of a credit card and not let it take advantage of you is another thing I would teach. You should never carry a balance on a credit card. It should essentially be used as a more safe version of a debit card, as it isn't directly connected to a checking account. If you don't have the money in your checking account to cover whatever you're paying on your credit card, then don't buy it. You can't afford it. This goes back to what some of my interviewees touched on regarding interest rates. The interest rate they charge you on the balance on a credit card is ridiculously high to prey on those who don't understand how interest works. I briefly brought this up earlier, but personal hygiene is something that I would want to emphasize. For many, it's not until high school or later that they really start to clean groom themselves properly and care about how they look and smell. This goes for oral hygiene, as well. Many neglect flossing, but it can go a long way to reduce or eliminate bad breath. Even something that may seem super simple, like finding a dentist or doctor after you've outgrown your pediatrician is worth teaching. It is true that in most cases no one notices as many things about you as yourself, it's always a good practice to put your best foot forward when you're in public. You never know who you may meet.

Tips

Tips for People Entering High School

In general, being yourself is seemingly the biggest tip my intervie-wees have for people about to go into high school. Don't be afraid to explore and express your creativity, as it will help you figure out what you want to do in the years to come. At the end of the day, high school is a very short period of your life, so don't treat it as the end-all, be-all. It's understandable to think that it was, as it is what you're experiencing right now, but just focus on getting through it if you find it difficult socially or academically. Try not to overthink things and focus on what matters most to you instead of what others say matters. At the same time, spend time with people with similar morals and values, as these people can become lifelong connections.

Tips for People Entering College

Your college experience is really dependent upon the effort you put in. To get ahead, just doing the coursework isn't enough. Take advantage of the opportunities your college provides you, as well as the general opportunities being in college provides. Internships, clubs, and mentorships are very valuable experiences. Explore your options. If you still don't know what you want to do, this is your time to take a step back and explore different majors and minors. Electives are a good way to dip your toe into things you think may interest you. The sooner in your college career you do this, the better. Once you've decided on what you want to do, truly try to absorb the information being taught. At the same time, some of the feedback from your professors will be subjective, rather than objective. Try your best to discern the difference and treat that feedback differently. Not everyone's opinion will work for you. Be open-minded and willing to accept things that are less than perfect. If you miss the mark because you try something different or are being creative, the learning experience is worth it. Again, this is your time to explore and test new ideas and approaches.

Tips for People Leaving College

It's not over. Yes, we've talked about trying to figure out what you want to do before you get here and have given some tips on how to do that. Still, when you graduate college, you're young and have time to figure that out through trial and error. You can still take chances and change your career many times. The sooner you figure out that you don't like what you're doing and move on to something else, the better. In whatever career you're in, whether you like it or not, try to be pleasant around your co-workers. They typically aren't the reason you don't like it, so they shouldn't have to deal with your negative attitude. Also, before you even get into a job, be proactive in your job search while you're still in college, at least a semester before you plan to graduate. Start to save money and figure out where you're going to live. These days, it's completely normal to continue to live with your parents for the early stages of your career. The delayed gratification of being able to move out with little financial burden or stress is well worth it. Delayed gratification, in general, is better than instant gratification. Things you work for over time always feel better.

Outro

Everyone is different. Some things come naturally to some people, and they don't need to be taught as much. It seems like my dad says just about everything came naturally to him. Others need every little detail spelled out to them. You know who you are and who you're dealing with. The goal of this wasn't to scold anyone or make this or that group feel bad. For the figures in authority, I wanted to give you somewhat of a guide of what today's young adults are missing from you. For the young adults, this is a similar guide, but giving you an idea of what you may want to ask or research for yourself. I know I didn't give all of the answers to everything that I brought up here. That wasn't my goal. I'm not an expert in taxes, finance, meditation, or anything really, so I don't want to give you poor advice in those arenas. I just want to get everyone thinking about how young adults are being brought up in today's world (at least in the US). Does anyone genuinely think that they have everything completely right? There's always room for improvement, so I wanted to give people some insight into what some young people think could be improved. With this information, people can go about filling in those gaps in whatever way they see fit. As long as an effort is made and that we acknowledge that these gaps exist and need to be filled, we should be on the right track. Many people hate to admit that they don't know something. By doing that, you're only preventing yourself, and potentially those around you, from knowing the truth. Hopefully, with this information, everyone becomes more curious. Curious about what you know that the younger person doesn't and vice versa. Over time, there should be fewer and fewer things they don't tell you, and more things you're glad they did.